Buster Posey

The Inspirational Story of Baseball Superstar Buster Posey

Table Of Contents

Introduction

As the title already implies, this is a book about [The Inspirational Story of Baseball Superstar Buster Posey] and how he rose from his life in Leesburg, Georgia to becoming one of today's leading and most-respected baseball players. In his rise to superstardom, Buster has inspired not only the youth, but fans of all ages, throughout the world.

This book also portrays the key moments that Buster has had to go through during his early childhood years, his teen years, and up until he became what he is today. A notable source of inspiration is Buster's service to the community and his strong connection with the fans of the sport. He continues to serve as the humble, hard-working superstar in a sport that needs positive role models.

Combining incredible strength, a strong throwing arm, high baseball IQ, and superior coordination, Buster has shown the ability to change the outcome of any game. From being a phenom man-child to becoming one of the greatest young ball players of his generation, you'll learn here how this man has risen to the ranks of the best baseball players today.

Thanks again for downloading this book. Hopefully you can take some of the examples from Buster's story and apply them to your own life!

Chapter 1:

Early Years

Born to Demp and Traci Posey on March 27th, 1987, Gerald Dempsey Posey III was the oldest of four children. Buster was a cherished family nickname given to his father and was later passed on to the him.

The Posey Athletes

Growing up with two brothers and a sister in the quiet town of Leesburg, Georgia, Buster and his siblings were always competitive and could routinely be seen playing at local sporting events. Buster's sister, Sam, even became a softball star with a fast pitching arm. The four Posey children grew up to be very talented athletes, but it was Buster who excelled in all four of the sports they played in – basketball, soccer, football, and baseball. Despite having natural abilities to excel in multiple sports, it was on the baseball field where Buster showed superstar potential at a young age, specifically through his extraordinary hitting and pitching skills.

Although he first played basketball, partly because his father was a player during college, Buster felt a certain attraction to baseball. He was so well-rounded that he played every position except catcher in the Minor Leagues and in small games at the Dixie Youth Baseball Fields.

The Protégé

Even at a young age, Buster showed excellent poise and a strong right arm, which easily stood out to his coaches. By the time he reached high school, Buster was already throwing fastballs in the 90 mile-per-hour range.

He played for the Trojans of Leesburg High School and was an athlete in multiple sports. Playing baseball never made academics difficult for Buster, as he was almost always in the top ten of his class. It was in Buster's sophomore year when scouts began to follow him as he played in All-Star tournaments. As a junior, Buster was invited to play in Taiwan as part of the United States Junior Olympic team.

Dominating opponents when he was on the mound with his fearsome fastball and improved batting skills at the plate, Buster led the LHS Trojans to the state championship with a .544 batting average and a 10-1 pitching record.

In his senior year, Buster hit for an average of .462 with only five strikeouts and 14 home runs under his belt. He also pitched a perfect 12-0 record with close to a 1.00 ERA. Due to his outstanding year, Buster was named Player of the Year for 2005 by Gatorade and was among the United States' top 20 high school prospects.

Universities and even some major league clubs were already making offers to him even before Buster had graduated high school. One intriguing offer came from Mike Martin, the baseball coach of Florida State University.

Mike's team had an amazing streak of 28 consecutive appearances at the NCAA Tournament. Some of Martin's top players had also gone on to become household names and two – J.D. Drew and Mike Lloyd – had been awarded the Golden Spikes award in their time at the University.

Buster decided to take up the offer and enroll at Florida State University to start playing ball for the Seminoles in 2005.

Chapter 2:

College Career

Buster's first position of his college baseball career was at shortstop, which he played at for his entire freshman year. For his first season, Buster hit for an average of .435 with four home runs and 48 RBI in 65 games played. The Seminoles finished with a 44-21 record, placing second in the Atlantic Coast Conference's Atlantic Division.

Buster was fortunate to play with talented players such power hitters Dennis Guinn and Jack Rye, as well as speeder, Shane Robinson. The starting pitching staff was led by Bryan Henry and Tyler Chambliss. Although the team made it back to the NCAA Tournament, they failed to get past the Regional round.

An Unlikely Shift

In 2007, Mike Martin Jr., FSU's assistant coach, suggested that Buster move from the shortstop position to catcher – a position unfamiliar to Buster, as he had never played it before. Martin Sr. was not fully sold on the idea because he believed that Buster's massive lower body would be more suitable to a corner position than catcher.

Although unusual, the move was similar to the conversion of Jorge Posada, an All-Star player who made the adjustment from middle infielder to catcher. Martin Jr. also made that same transition during his baseball playing days in college.

The idea was brought up near the end of 2006 and Buster agreed to it immediately. Martin Jr. was sure that the move to catcher would not only help the Seminoles, but also increase Buster's appeal to the big league teams. It proved to be helpful as it addressed FSU's obvious handicap as the team headed into 2007.

Testing The Waters

To see if Buster would adjust well to the catcher position, one of the team's first games for that season was an exhibition game against the Philadelphia Phillies. After an easy win by the Seminoles, the Phillies' coach, Charlie Manuel, approached Martin Sr. and told him something that would mean a great deal. He said the best player that day was a sophomore who'd only been a catcher for a few weeks, and it was an eye-opening experience for him.

Buster quickly adjusted to the new position and showed excellent catching skills almost immediately, so much so that he was named a Johnny Bench Award finalist – the first ever for a sophomore. This was also largely due to his second superb season at the plate. For the season, Buster hit for an average of .382 with 65 RBI. He even got the chance to meet Bench himself, who is considered by many to be the greatest catcher of all-time.

For the 30th straight year, FSU made it to the NCAA Tournament, banking on its 24-6 conference record, which was atop the ACC. The

Seminoles finished with a ranking of 16th in the nation and had a 49-13 overall record. However, they were unfortunately unable to win a national championship. Nonetheless, 2007 was a great year overall for the team, as well as for Buster's development as a catcher.

Honing The Home Run Stroke

At the start of the 2008 season, it seemed that Buster only had one weakness, the home run stroke. To combat this, Buster went to work in the offseason to develop his bat speed and swinging power and the results paid off during the season.

Buster was crushing the ball no matter where his opponents pitched to him; not only resulting in home runs, but his overall slugging ability was also helping to knock in baserunners. It was during this season that Buster nearly pulled off the rarest feat in college baseball – winning the NCAA Triple Crown. He led the Seminoles with an average of .463 to go along with 93 RBI.

He was also just two home runs away from a total of 28, a record set by NCAA legends Matt Clark and Gordon Beckham. Buster also topped all hitters with a .566 on-base percentage, 226 total bases, and 119 hits. It seemed as though the hard work that Buster put in was really starting to   pay   off.

One Was Not Enough

In the second half of his college career, Buster practically dominated college baseball, making other players seem like high school athletes. He was impossible to strike out and on several occasions when the team needed an important victory, Buster took from the field to the mound and earned a save. His 1.17 ERA on the team remains unchallenged to this day.

Florida State University won 54 games and for the first time since 2001, reached the College World Series. Throughout the tournament, Buster went 8-for-16 with five home runs and 13 RBI when the Seminoles were on the brink of elimination.

Unfortunately, Florida State lost twice in the College World Series, ending its dream of winning a national championship. This proved that having one power player, even someone as excellent as Buster, was not enough to help the Florida State Seminoles get the CWS championship they had been longing for.

However, the loss didn't affect Buster's snowballing fame. Trophies and accolades were pouring in from everywhere and he was gaining recognition quickly. He virtually won all the Player of the Year awards, including the Dick Howser Trophy and the Golden Spikes award. FSU fans even sang a song created just for him, entitled "Hail to the Buster", whenever he stepped in to bat.

The Draft

Even though he had less experience than most draftees, Buster was already regarded as the top catcher prospect in the MLB Draft. As a result, the San Francisco Giants selected him with the fifth overall pick. Two college players, slugger Pedro Alvarez from Vanderbilt, and lefty Brian Matusz from San Diego, were chosen ahead of him.

Upon being drafted, Buster leveraged his remaining one year of eligibility in college to negotiate with the San Francisco Giants. Before the signing deadline in August, the Giants offered Buster a bonus of $6.2 million dollars. At the time, it was $100,000 dollars more than what was received by Justin Upton and it was the highest in history for such a situation. During the winter of that same year, Buster married his high school sweetheart, Kristin. She took care of the paperwork while Buster was preparing for spring training.

Chapter 3:

Professional Career

Buster was initially assigned to the Class-A Team of the San Francisco Giants to start the 2009 season. The team was located in San Jose, about 45 minutes south of San Francisco. During his stay with the team, Buster hit .336 as well as 13 home runs in just half the season.

He was then promoted to the Fresno Grizzlies, a Class-AAA team to continue his development. Buster showed no signs of slowing down as he hit .321 with 5 home runs in 121 at-bats. Finally, in early September of 2009, Buster was called up to join the Giants in the major league.

Major League Debut

Already on its way to an 88-win season, the San Francisco Giants were having a difficult time pushing through the powerful NL West. Although the team had great pitching talents in Tim Lincecum, Brian Wilson, Matt Cain, and Jonathan Sanchez, it lacked punch on the offensive side.

At that time, Bengie Molina, the team's most experienced hitter, was also the starting catcher. Buster made his first professional appearance at the major league level on September 11th, 2009. However, the manager, Bruce Bochy, did not limit Buster's starts to catcher. Buster was doing well when he was behind the plate but struggled in the batter's box. He only collected a pair of singles in his first 17 at-bats.

That seemingly lackluster major league debut performance sent Buster back to the minor leagues in 2010, playing again for the Fresno Grizzlies. This demotion could have easily made Buster pessimistic about his future, but he never gave up and continued to work towards his dream. Thanks to the work ethic that he learned in his youth, Buster kept grinding to prove that he could become a successful major league player one day. All he needed to do was show his worth and wait for the next opportunity to present itself.

Meanwhile, the Giants continued to drift deeper down the NL West standings because of their lack of power hitting. Then things turned upside down in the following season, the lowly San Diego Padres were off to a great start, the Los Angeles Dodgers began to struggle, and the Colorado Rockies were performing unpredictably.

The Giants kept patient and hit, fielded, and pitched just well enough to keep afloat and stay within striking distance of San Diego. As spring turned to summer, the team was able to come up with a decent offense by adding Cody Ross, Jose Guillen, and Pat Burrell. Veterans Andres Torres, Juan Uribe, and Aubrey Huff also showed surprising performances when handed leading roles by Bochy.

Back To The Majors

In the months of April and May, the Giants were getting unsatisfactory production from the corner infield positions so Bochy decided to call Buster back up. The plan was to have Buster play a little at each of the corner positions. The team was hoping that he could learn and also contribute as soon as possible. Buster did not disappoint them.

When playing against the Arizona Diamondbacks in his first couple of games, Buster collected three hits. He then followed this up with a hitting streak of 10 straight games, while also hitting his first major league home run when the Giants played the Cincinnati Reds.

By this point, Buster had completely shaken off the major league jitters and was getting respect from the opposing pitchers. He adjusted almost immediately to any change in the pitching approach and was hitting with confidence. Buster also proved that he was more than a competent catcher and showed great chemistry with the pitching staff. By the end of June, following Molina's trade, Buster became the team's designated starting catcher.

The Injury

Although essentially a non-contact sport, accidents can and do happen on the baseball field. Unfortunately, the inevitable happened to Buster in a collision that would threaten to end his career. On May 25th, 2011, Buster was involved in a brutal collision with Scott Cousins of the Florida Marlins as the latter was going towards home plate in a 6-6 deadlocked game. The San Francisco Giants lost the game and Buster was left writhing in pain while the fans and his teammates were silent and worried.

After several minutes of confusion, the fans started chanting Buster's name and two Giants trainers helped him stand up while another one was holding his left leg up. It was a sad moment and Buster looked stunned as he was being helped off the field.

With a broken ankle bone and damage to his ligaments, Buster had no choice but to end his season in order to recover from the injury. But the effect of his injury extended beyond the physical, as the lack of an excellent catcher on the team led sports critics wondering how the

Giants would fare without him. Buster, with his outstanding performances and endearing charm, had also been the face of the Giants franchise since he stepped in and fans were left hanging without their main star.

The Comeback

Getting back on the baseball field after suffering a fractured fibula, a completely dislocated left ankle, and three torn ligaments would not be a walk in the park and Buster knew it. But with the help of his teammates and the constant inspiration from the fans, Buster went through a couple of surgeries, months of rehabilitation, and the daily pains of scratching the scar tissue. Once again, Buster would need to dig deep and have to work extremely hard in order to make it back to his playing form. This could have really hurt his confidence, but Buster stayed the course.

His return to the field after being out for almost a year was met with anticipation and excitement, as Buster stepped in against the Reds in March of 2012. Surprisingly, the injury didn't seem to slow down the San Francisco Giants star catcher as he continued his stellar performances.

He proved to critics that he could not only come back, but become even better, after suffering the horrific injury. To top it all of, Buster caught every inning during the playoffs and led the

Giants to a World Series Championship and was also awarded the National League's Most Valuable Player Award as well as the Comeback Player of the Year Award. These achievements proved to everyone that Buster was back and here to stay.

Chapter 4:

Up Close and Personal

Even at the peak of his baseball career and fame, Buster Posey has remained grounded. The Giant's superstar is also very private when it comes to his life away from the diamond. This is one of the reasons why he and his wife, Kristen, together with their twin sons and a daughter, decided to build their home in the hills of Lamorinda, where they can always find peace and quiet away from the noise.

Charity Work

Growing up in the quiet town of Leesburg in a closely knit family, Buster learned the importance of sharing with those that are less fortunate. This has been shown in the several charity activities that he's supported and continues to support.

In his latest and much talked about contract with the San Francisco Giants, in which he signed a $167 million deal that would span nine years, Buster agreed to donate $50,000 annually to charities that the Giants were involved with. This would be almost half a million dollars of donations for the duration of his contract.

The San Francisco Giants in their community and charity activities support helpful programs such as providing scholarships to deserving students, and raising sports and education awareness. They also provide grants to approved non-profit organizations.

On October 26th, 2010, Major League Baseball gave Buster Posey the Player's Choice Award and the National League named him Rookie of the Year. As part of his award, Buster was given the opportunity to choose a cause or charity to which $20,000 would be donated.

He decided to give the amount to 19 For Life. 19 for Life is a non-profit foundation established in the memory of DJ Frandsen, brother of ex-Giants hitter, Kevin Frandsen. The organization provides funding for activities for sick children at the Lucile Packard Children's Hospital, scholarships for athletes at the local community high schools, and seniors from Bellarmine who need financial assistance to finish their high school education.

The Heart of San Francisco

With his consistent stellar performances and mild mannered character, Buster is easy to root for and a great ambassador for the sport of baseball.

But even with all of his fame and the attention of millions of baseball fans, this Giant has remained soft-spoken, humble and down to earth. He's kept his private life out of public consumption and has managed to keep that endearing character even during the heat of a baseball game.

His success and persona have made Buster one of the most loved icons in baseball. Buster has an especially large fan base when it comes to the youth. Many teenagers can relate to him and root for him after seeing him overcome incredible odds in his short time on earth.

Lesser Known Facts About Buster

Once in a game at Florida State, Buster played all nine positions, struck out two batters, and then hit grand slam. He led the Seminoles to a 10-0 victory against Savannah State, using four different gloves during the game.

Buster's favorite show is History Channel's Swamp People, which he watches with his wife. They also watch The Bachelorette, Kristen's favorite. Kristen is Buster's high school sweetheart and they were married in January of 2009.

At exactly nine months after the day he led the Giants to winning the World Series in 2010, Lee Dempsey and Addison Lynn, his twin sons, were born.

At 23 years old, Buster was the youngest player from the Giants to hit a home run during the World Series.

Buster's young sister, Samantha, was a softball star and played for Valdosa State.

Chapter 5:

Career Summary and Milestones

Here is a list of a few of Buster's career accomplishments and milestones in his short career:

Played for the USA Junior Olympic Team as Pitcher

Awarded Georgia's Gatorade Player of the Year Award

Awarded the Golden Spikes and the Dick Howser Trophy

Post-Season All-Star (Hawaii Winter Baseball 11/16/2008)

Player of the Week (California League 04/20/2009)

Mid-Season All-Star (California League 06/23/2009)

Player of the Year (Topps/Minor League 10/28/2009)

Rising Stars (Arizona Fall League 11/02/2009)

Prospect Team (Arizona Fall League 12/09/2009)

Player of the Week (National League 07/12/2010)

Rookie of the Month (National League 07/31/2010)

Clutch Performer of the Month (Major League Baseball 07/31/2010)

Player of the Month (National League 07/31/2010)

Players' Choice Award (Major League Baseball 10/26/2010)

Outstanding Rookie (National League 10/26/2010)

World Series Champion (11/01/2010)

Rookie of the Year Award (National League 11/15/2010)

Comeback Player of the Year Award (National League 10/19/2012)

Hank Aaron Award (National League 10/27/2012)

World Series Champion (10/28/2012)

Players' Choice Award (Major League Baseball 11/05/2012)

Comeback Player of the Year Award (National League 11/05/2012)

Silver Slugger (National League 11/08/2012)

Most Valuable Player Award (National League 11/08/2012)

Player of the Week (National League 07/01/2013)

Conclusion

I hope this book was able to help you to gain inspiration from the life of Buster Posey, one of the best players currently playing in Major League Baseball.

The rise and fall of a star is often the cause for much wonder. But most stars have an expiration date. In baseball, once a star player reaches his mid- to late-thirties, it is often time to contemplate retirement. What will be left in people's minds about that fading star? In Buster Posey's case, people will remember how he came onto the scene for the Giants and recovered from a gruesome injury. He will be remembered as the guy who helped his team build their image by winning multiple championships, while building his own image along the way.

Quiet, laid-back, and shy, this San Francisco Giants catcher has baseball fans in awe with a playing prowess that sportswriters say is comparable to that of the legendary, Joe

DiMaggio. Coupled with a square jaw, a commanding height of 6 feet and 1 inch, and a boy-next-door smile, he's baseball card material for sure.

Buster has also inspired so many people because he is the star who never fails to connect with fans and gives back to the less fortunate. Noted for his ability to impose his will on any game, he is a joy to watch on the baseball field. Last but not least, he's remarkable for remaining simple and firm with his principles in spite of his immense popularity.

Hopefully you learned some great things about Buster in this book and are able to apply some of the lessons that you've learned to your own life! Good luck!

Other Athlete Stories That Will Inspire You!

Mike Trout

http://www.amazon.com/dp/B00HKKCNNU

Miguel Cabrera

http://www.amazon.com/dp/B00HKG3G1W

Lou Gehrig

http://www.amazon.com/dp/B00KOZMONW

Babe Ruth

http://www.amazon.com/dp/B00IS2YB48

Floyd Mayweather

http://www.amazon.com/dp/B00HLEX5O6

Anderson Silva

http://www.amazon.com/dp/BooHLBOVVU

Inspirational Football Stories!

Peyton Manning

http://www.amazon.com/dp/B00HJUYTCY

Tom Brady

http://www.amazon.com/dp/B00HJYQTRS

Aaron Rodgers

http://www.amazon.com/dp/B00HJUEDEI

Colin Kaepernick

http://www.amazon.com/dp/B00IRHHABU

Russell Wilson

http://www.amazon.com/dp/B00HK909C8

Calvin Johnson

http://www.amazon.com/dp/B00HJK0YS2

Inspirational Basketball Stories!

Stephen Curry

http://www.amazon.com/dp/B00HH9QU1A

Derrick Rose

http://www.amazon.com/dp/B00HH1BE82

Blake Griffin

http://www.amazon.com/dp/B00INNVVIG

Carmelo Anthony

http://www.amazon.com/dp/B00HH9L3P8

Chris Paul

http://www.amazon.com/dp/B00HIZXMSW

Paul George

http://www.amazon.com/dp/B00IN3YIVI

Dirk Nowitzki

http://www.amazon.com/dp/B00HRVPD9I

Kevin Durant

http://www.amazon.com/dp/B00HIKDK34

46187936R00033

Made in the USA
Lexington, KY
26 October 2015